W9-DGY-725

LEE CANTER'S

parent conference book

LEE CANTER WITH BARBARA SCHADLOW

CANTER & ASSOCIATES, INC.

Lee Canter's Parent Conference Book Copyright ©1984 by Lee Canter. All rights reserved. Printed in the United States of America. No part of this book may be used or reproduced in any manner whatsoever without the prior written consent of the publisher. For information address Canter & Associates, Inc., 1553 Euclid Street, Santa Monica, California 90404.

FIRST EDITION

ISBN 0-9608978-4-4

A publication of Canter & Associates, Inc., developers of Assertive Discipline.

2nd printing August 1985
3rd printing August 1986
4th printing March 1987

TABLE OF CONTENTS

Why You Need This Book

Phyllis Roberts unlocked the door. She flicked on the light and looked around. It was strange to see darkness through the windows. How different it was to be in her classroom at night. But something was wrong. She glanced at her watch. Only ten minutes to go! She began racing through the room dragging chairs from the tops of desks and banging them to the floor. Why didn't I have the kids leave their chairs *down* this one afternoon?

Five minutes later, out of breath, Phyllis looked around again. Chairs down, desks clear, blackboard clean, bulletin boards neat. This was an important night, and she wanted everything to be perfect. She composed herself, took two deep breaths and sat at her desk. A smile crossed her lips; she was ready.

It was Parent Conference Night, and she was eager to meet her students' parents.

The first to arrive was Mrs. Green, Johnny's mother. Johnny was the most difficult child in the class. He was severely disruptive, and a poor student as well. Phyllis had been warned about Mrs. Green from his teacher last year. Mrs. Green had a reputation throughout the school of being extremely uncooperative.

Suddenly Phyllis' enthusiasm for meeting her students' parents was gone. Instead she was overcome by a sinking feeling in the pit of her stomach. She was not prepared for an encounter with Mrs. Green.

She ushered Mrs. Green to the chair next to her desk. Mrs. Green lowered herself onto the child-sized chair, looked up at Phyllis and frowned.

Phyllis' head began to spin. There were so many problems that needed to be discussed. Where should she begin? What should she say? She opened her mouth to speak, but no words came out.

1

This meeting and hundreds more like it take place in classrooms throughout this country. The intentions are honorable on each side. Both teacher and parent want Johnny to do better in school, but communication is so poor between them that the meeting does not produce results. Instead it becomes a polite chat or an uncomfortable confrontation.

There are many reasons why Phyllis Roberts, the teacher in our example, felt intimidated by her meeting with Mrs. Green. For one thing, she was unprepared to discuss Johnny's problems. She had no documentation of the child's misbehavior, nor had she planned ahead of time what she would say.

Furthermore, she had not contacted Mrs. Green earlier when the problems first began. She had tried her best to deal with Johnny on her own and though she was unsuccessful, she had never approached his mother for help. Now his behavior was out of hand and she was faced with breaking the bad news to an unsuspecting parent.

Phyllis Roberts did what many teachers do. She viewed her involvement with parents as limited to twice-a-year parent-teacher conferences and report card time. Due to a lack of skills she avoided contact with difficult parents and spoke with them only if they came to school during conference time. That was her big mistake.

Fortunately, most of the parents you meet throughout your teaching career are not like Mrs. Green. Most parents are eager to support you and welcome your guidance in dealing with their children. However, there may be a handful who are reluctant to cooperate. Your communication with those parents may be ineffective and leave you feeling frustrated and helpless. But keep in mind that in order to do the best job possible, you must gain the support of those parents, too.

This book will help you do that. It will help you develop a total plan for positive parent communication, the premise being that communication with parents is an on-going process - one that begins the first day of school and continues throughout the year.

By following the guidelines presented in this book, you will be able to break down the barriers between you and the difficult parents you meet throughout your teaching career. You will develop the skills and confidence to approach parents whenever there is a problem. And within a short time, you will be able to gain the support of all parents, and parent-teacher conferences will be easier than ever before.

Though this book was originally designed to aid teachers in working more effectively with difficult parents, it will greatly enhance your ability to communicate with all your students' parents. Furthermore, the suggestions offered in the book are geared primarily to students with behavior problems, simply because teachers have a harder time communicating with parents in relation to behavior. However, the same techniques can be applied to academic problems.

Obstacles to Parental Support

For the past 14 years we have been working with teachers throughout the country. We have studied the ways in which they communicate with parents. We have found that there are three major obstacles preventing many teachers, and which may prevent you, from dealing more effectively with parents.

Non-Supportive Parents

Parents today are not as supportive as they were in the past. Changes in the political and social climate in our country have widened the gap between parents and teachers. Many parents question the teachers' capabilities while others are outwardly antagonistic or hostile. The teaching profession does not command the respect it once did.

The situation was a lot different when we were in school. Ask yourself this: Why did we behave when we were students? The answer is simple. We knew that our parents would give their total support to our teachers if we were out of line. Teachers were spoken of with reverence and highly regarded for their wisdom.

Today, however, teachers encounter parents who say:

"My daughter is your problem from 9:00 to 3:00. Don't bother me."

"Look, I'm a single parent. I'm too busy to be bothered with my children's behavior in school. I have enough trouble making them toe the line when they're home."

"I work full time. I can just about see to it that my kids eat dinner at night and get to bed on time."

The Myth Of The Good Teacher

Many teachers feel that the student's entire well-being - educational, social, physical and emotional - is their responsibility from 9:00 till 3:00. These teachers labor under the misguided belief that in order to be a "good teacher" they should be able to handle all problems on their own within the confines of the classroom. What an unrealistic burden for the teacher who has thirty students or more to instruct!

Such teachers feel incompetent if they ask parents for support. They regard approaching parents as a sign of failure. This results in many teachers avoiding asking parents for help or approaching parents in an ineffective or "beaten" manner.

Teachers Lack Skills In Dealing Effectively With Parents

The third obstacle preventing teachers from gaining parental support is that education classes did not provide training in communicating with parents. Teacher training classes basically assumed that parents would be totally cooperative and offer support in any way, shape, or form deemed necessary. Given the reality of today's students and parents, it is an absurd assumption. Without specific skills, you will not be able to deal effectively with many of today's parents. Without an organized procedure, you will not be able to gain the support of all of your students' parents.

What Happens Without Training

Lack of training leaves many teachers unprepared for communicating effectively with parents. Therefore, without training, teachers generally approach difficult situations with parents in one of two ineffective ways.

They Avoid Contact

When a student misbehaves or displays academic problems, many teachers bear the burden of the problem themselves and avoid all contact with parents. From past experience they assume that the parent won't help them, so why try?

Most often the problem escalates and the teacher becomes more frustrated. When it reaches the point at which the student is in jeopardy of failing or of being suspended, the teacher finally calls the parent to school.

The common reaction from the parent is: "Why didn't you tell me about Susie's problem sooner?" The parent may become angry, and rightly so. "I could have done something about it. Now it's too late."

Once burnt from a situation like this, the teacher does anything to avoid a replay. Therefore, the next time the student misbehaves, the teacher avoids calling the parents, and the cycle repeats itself.

They Use a Non-Assertive Approach.

Other teachers deal with uncooperative parents in a vague, passive, wishy-washy fashion. We call this a "non-assertive" approach.

Due to a lack of skills and confidence, some teachers do not clearly state what problem the student is having and what help is needed from parents. Instead teachers...

- Minimize the problem
  "We had a small problem with your son today." (In reality, he had a violent tantrum which disrupted the entire class for 15 minutes.)

- Belittle their abilities
  "I just don't know what to do with your son." (In fact, the teacher does know what to do. The cooperation of the parents is needed to discipline him at home for his tantrums.)

- Downgrade the consequences of the student's behavior

6

"I don't know what will happen if he doesn't change his behavior in class." (Yes, the teacher does know the outcome. The student will be suspended.)

This type of non-assertive approach is ineffective because it rarely produces results - the student remains a problem and the teacher does not have the parents' support.

The Assertive Teacher

Though some teachers are ineffective in working with parents, there are a number of teachers who are successful in gaining parental support. These teachers approach all parents, even the most difficult ones, in a firm, confident and straightforward manner. We call this effective way of dealing with parents an "assertive" approach.

You, too, can become more effective and increase the probability of your success with parents simply by acquiring the attitude and skills that assertive teachers possess. The two key concepts to remember are:

Assume a take-charge attitude when dealing with parents

Develop a systematic plan before contacting parents

Assume a Take-Charge Attitude

Assertive teachers have the attitude: "I have a right to parental support." They operate with the assumption that they need and deserve parental support. They believe it is in the student's best interest, in the class's best interest, and in their best interest that the

7

parents take responsibility for their children's behavior. They have the attitude: "I cannot do my job alone. If a student stops me from teaching, his or her parents must become involved." These teachers make no exceptions. No matter how difficult a parent has been in the past, these teachers demand support and stop at nothing to get it.

To better understand this take-charge attitude think about another professional who deals with children - a pediatrician.

A pediatrician approaches parents in a firm, direct, matter-of-fact manner. He or she diagnoses the illness, tells the parent what medication to administer, the parent cooperates, and the child recovers. Underlying a pediatrician's words is the attitude: "I am a professional. I studied for many years and know what is best for your child's health. I expect you to follow my suggestions."

Likewise, you, the educator, must approach parents with a similar attitude: "I know how your child can best achieve in school. This is what I recommend. I expect you to support me."

Develop a Systematic Plan

As we said before, communication with parents should not be limited to twice-a-year routine parent-teacher conferences. You must establish positive communication with parents early in the school year and keep them informed throughout the year, especially when there is a problem.

In order to communicate with parents most effectively, we have devised a simple, systematic plan. The plan includes a few, step-by-step procedures plus the use of specific written and verbal skills.

Once these procedures and skills are part of your professional routine, you will have the confidence to approach all parents - even the most difficult ones and ask for their help. With parental support your students' behavior will improve and you will be better able to do what you were hired to do - teach!

8

The next part of this book helps you develop the systematic plan you must use to become more confident and assertive with parents.

I. Establish classroom standards.
Parents need to feel you deal with their children in a fair, consistent manner. In order to do so, you must determine the standards (behavioral and academic) in your classroom. What are the rules in your class? What are the consequences for breaking those rules? What must a child do that would prompt you to call the parents? How do you expect the parents to support you?

II. Communicate standards to parents.
If you expect parental support, you must communicate your classroom standards to them. They must know what you expect from their children and how they must support you.

III. Establish positive communication.
You must be in continual communication with parents. You should let them know about their children's commendable behavior and achievement in school. Parents need to perceive that you have a positive attitude toward their child.

IV. Document all problems.
In order to present an accurate picture of a child's problem, you must document all inappropriate behavior. This documentation will enable you to give parents a professional, nonjudgmental account of their child's behavior.

V. Contact parents at the first sign of a problem.
When a problem arises and you must contact parents, prepare for the phone call or meeting. You must plan what you will say, how you will say it, and what you will do if the parents won't support you. You will also need to develop skills that can be used if parents attempt to sidetrack or manipulate you.

VI. When all else fails.
You may encounter children with severe problems and parents who absolutely refuse to support you. For these cases you must be prepared to utilize firm measures to gain parental support.

In the next section, we will discuss each procedure in detail, giving specific examples, ideas and tips for implementation to insure success.

PROCEDURE

I

ESTABLISH CLASSROOM STANDARDS

ESTABLISH CLASSROOM STANDARDS

To lay the foundation for gaining parental support, you must first determine the standards for your classroom.

- What behaviors do you expect of your students?
- What academic achievements must be attained?
- What will you do if a student does not meet your standards?
- How will you reinforce students who do meet your standards?
- Which behaviors do you want parents to support?

You can best lay this foundation by devising a discipline plan for your classroom. Just as you prepare lessons for reading, math or science, you should formulate a discipline plan. And do it before the first day of school. Having well-defined standards and pre-determined consequences from the very beginning will assist you in your teaching efforts and give you a basis for effectively communicating with parents. You will be able to:

- Judge student behavior fairly
- Discuss behavior problems more confidently with parents and administrators.

Your reasons for calling a parent will never be vague or arbitrary. You can accurately describe to a parent:

- The rules that the student has broken
- The consequences of the student's misbehavior

13

Once your discipline plan has been formulated, you should communicate your standards to your class. Your students must know exactly what is expected of them. They can then make a choice: Follow the rules and enjoy the rewards or accept the consequences of disregarding the rules.

Be sure to share the discipline plan with your administrator. Having administrative support will increase your effectiveness with both students and parents.

> **TIP**
> It is important that rules are visible at all times. Write them on a poster and display them prominently in the classroom.

Sample Discipline Plan

Many effective educators utilize the guidelines of the Assertive Discipline* program for setting up discipline plans. Teachers prepare plans suitable for their needs in the classroom, and administrators oversee a similar schoolwide plan to cover behavior in the common areas of the cafeteria, yard and halls.

The discipline plan should include:

- A set of rules that are in effect at all times in your classroom or school

- The negative consequences you will provide for students who do not follow the rules

- How you will positively reinforce students who do follow the rules

---

*Refer to Lee Canter's *Assertive Discipline - A Take-Charge Approach for Today's Educator* and *Assertive Discipline Resource Materials and Guidelines* for specific techniques for setting up a discipline plan.

Here is an example of a classroom discipline plan:

I. Class Rules:

Follow directions.
Keep hands, feet, objects to yourself.
No talking without permission.
No cussing or teasing.
Have all work assignments finished
on time.

II. If a student breaks a rule:

1st consequence: Warning,
(name on blackboard)
2nd consequence: Check after name,
15 minutes after school
3rd consequence: Two checks after name,
30 minutes after school
4th consequence: Four checks after name,
30 minutes after school, call parents
5th consequence: Four checks after name,
30 minutes after school, call parents,
send to another class for one hour
Severe clause: Send to principal

III. Students who comply with the rules receive:

Praise
Positive notes home
Stars or stickers
Small rewards
Class parties
Special events

15

WORKSHEET — Use this worksheet to formulate a discipline plan.

I. List the rules for your classroom or school.
(Keep them simple, specific and in observable terms)

RULE 1 _____
RULE 2 _____
RULE 3 _____
RULE 4 _____
RULE 5 _____

II. Determine the negative consequences for students who break the rules.

First time a student breaks a rule _____
Second time _____
Third time _____
Fourth time _____
Fifth time _____

What is the consequence for students who exhibit severe misbehavior?
_____
_____

III. Decide upon positive consequences to reinforce students who follow the rules.

praise _____
_____
_____
_____
_____

PROCEDURE

II

COMMUNICATE STANDARDS TO PARENTS

COMMUNICATE STANDARDS TO PARENTS

If you expect parents to support you, you must communicate to them the classroom standards you want them to support.

One of the key skills that effective teachers possess is the ability to clearly and firmly communicate to parents what support is needed. These teachers communicate with parents on the first day of school by sending home a letter outlining the rules and consequences of their discipline plan. Such a letter states in very straightforward and specific terms how they manage their classroom and what help they need from parents.

> TIP
> Educational experts have conducted studies to determine how parents judge competency in teachers. The studies show that two of the leading qualities of master teachers, according to parents, are:
> The ability to discipline
> The desire to work with parents

Keep these guidelines in mind when you write the letter to parents:

- State your philosophy of education
  "Every student has a right to learn and no student will prevent another student from learning."

- Express your expectations of students (behavioral and/or academic) in specific terms.
  "I expect all students to be ready to work when the bell rings."

- Explain how you will deal with students who misbehave.
  "Students who choose to break the rules will miss recess."

- Describe the positive feedback you will provide for students who do behave.
  "If students follow the rules they will be rewarded with praise, free time, etc."

- Communicate to parents that you need their support.
  "In order for your child to have the optimum learning experience, I will need your support."

- Provide a space on the letter for parents to write comments to you about their children.

- Ask parents to sign the tear-off portion of the letter and return it to you.

> TIP
> Keep the signed tear-off in the child's folder to verify that parents are aware of and support your discipline efforts.

> TIP
> Do not limit the letter to discipline standards. Include your academic expectations too.
> "There will be a homework assignment every night and a spelling test on Friday."
> Parents need to know what work their children are expected to do at home in order to supervise them properly.
> If you have a conference with a parent about a child's poor work habits and question the lack of supervision at home, the parent cannot claim ignorance of the assignments. You have the signed letter to prove the parent has been informed of your policy.

IMPORTANT: Some parents may not agree with your educational philosophy and refuse to sign the letter. In such cases, suggest a meeting with the parent and include the principal. Explain that you cannot adequately do your job without parental support and the child will not receive the optimum educational opportunity.

If the parent still refuses to sign, he or she must be made aware that whether or not the letter is signed, the child is still subject to the same rules and consequences as the rest of the class.

In extreme cases, it may be in the child's best interest that he or she be transferred to another class.

Dear Parents:

I am pleased to have your child in my class this year. In order to guarantee your child and all the students in my classroom the excellent educational climate they deserve, I will tolerate no student stopping me from teaching nor any student stopping another from learning.

Therefore, in my classroom I am utilizing the following discipline plan:

Rules:

Follow directions.
Be in your seat ready to work when the bell rings.
Raise your hand to speak and wait to be called upon.
Hand in all assignments on time.
Keep hands, feet and objects to yourself.

If a student chooses to break a rule:

1st consequence: Name on board, warning
2nd consequence: One check, lose 15 minutes of recess
3rd consequence: Two checks, lose 30 minutes of recess
4th consequence: Three checks, lose 30 minutes of recess, parents called
5th consequence: Four checks, lose 30 minutes of recess, parents called,
                 student sent to principal

Severe Disruption: Send immediately to principal.

Students who behave appropriately will be positively rewarded with:
positive notes home   praise   free time
bonus points   class parties

It is in your child's best interest that we work together with regard to his or her schooling. I will thus keep you informed about your child's progress in my class.

I have already discussed this plan with your child, but would appreciate it if you would review it with him or her before signing and returning the form below.

Thank you for your support.

Sincerely,

Please sign and return this portion.

Parent/Guardian Signature _____

Child's Name _____

Date _____

Comments

_____

_____

24

REMEMBER: Parents appreciate receiving a letter the first day of school. It shows them that:

- You're committed to the job of educating their children

- You've already done a great deal of planning for this class

- You have a strong disciplinary code

PROCEDURE

III

ESTABLISH POSITIVE COMMUNICATION

ESTABLISH POSITIVE COMMUNICATION

Parents are accustomed to hearing from the school only when their child has misbehaved or is doing poorly. It's not surprising, then, that some parents have a negative view toward teachers and the school system. You can change that attitude by providing consistent positive feedback and establishing a positive atmosphere in your classroom from the very beginning. This positive approach will also increase your probability of gaining parental support when problems do arise.

Our experience tells us that:

- Parents are more apt to support teachers who have a positive attitude toward students.

- Parents view the ability to praise students as an important quality of a competent teacher.

Therefore, begin to positively reinforce students immediately. And have some fun with it! We in education are often bogged down by rules, deadlines, reading scores, accountability and countless other serious issues, forgetting about the lighter side of education - the side that probably made us choose this profession in the first place -that we enjoy being with kids and receive satisfaction from educating them.

TIP
Make it a habit to send home two positive notes a day and to call one parent per week.

29

So the next key skill we present to you is the one that will stimulate smiles and good feelings - that is: **PROVIDE STUDENTS WITH POSITIVE FEEDBACK FOR A JOB WELL DONE.**

Effective teachers use a wide variety of ways to reward students who behave or do good work. They have an endless supply of positive notes, stickers, stars, stamps and prizes, as well as words of praise, positive gestures and symbols. To use this skill most effectively, you must go out of your way to find students who are following the rules. In other words **CATCH THEM DOING SOMETHING GOOD.** This is especially easy at the beginning of the school year when most students are on their best behavior.

> **TIP**
> Prepare notes ahead of time for each student. Preaddress envelopes too. Then, as you catch your students following the rules, just put the notes into the mail.

Once you see a student doing something right and reward them, carry it one step further and include the parents in on the good news. What a treat it will be for the parents to receive some positive words for a change. Either send home a quick note for a student's good behavior or academic work, or set aside a few minutes after school or in the evening for a few short phone calls. (SEE SAMPLE)

> **TIP**
> When writing notes, address the parents by name, and mention the student's name too. Keep the notes brief and to the point.

30

> TIP
> Look through last year's records for students who are known to have problems. Catch them doing something good immediately and let their parents know. It may prevent any problems from occuring at all!

REMEMBER: Positive feedback increases the probability that students will not misbehave. In a classroom situation children look for an adult's attention. If they don't get it for doing the right thing, they are bound to do the wrong thing!

Example: Notes

Dear Dr. and Mrs. Robbins,
It is my pleasure to tell you that Donna received an A on her first chemistry quiz. If she keeps up the good work, she will do very well this year.
Sincerely,
Mr. Ellis

Dear Ms. Arnold:
I am pleased to have Jackie in my class. She completed all of her work this week and was very well behaved. You should feel proud!
Sincerely,
Ms. Harrison

Dear Mr. and Mrs. Smith,
Larry puts away all of his toys at cleanup times. He follows the classroom rules and plays nicely with other children.
He is a lovely boy.
Sincerely,
Mrs. Linden

Sample Phone Conversation

Teacher:	Hello, Ms. Kelly. This is Ms. Jones, Mike's teacher.
Ms. Kelly:	What did he do wrong?
Teacher:	Mike didn't do anything wrong. As a matter of fact, I'm calling to tell you that he's done very well this first week of school. He did all of his classwork and handed in all homework assignments.
Ms. Kelly:	I can't believe you're calling me to tell me he's doing well. I'm so used to hearing bad things about Mike.
Teacher:	I believe it's just as important to tell parents when their child is doing well in school as it is when they're doing poorly.
Ms. Kelly:	I wish all teachers were like you.
Teacher:	I'd just like to add that I am pleased to have your son in my class and look forward to working with you to insure that he gets the most out of this school year.

PROCEDURE

IV

DOCUMENT ALL PROBLEMS

DOCUMENT ALL PROBLEMS

A positive approach works very well with most students, but there will be a few who remain continual behavior problems from the beginning. In order to present parents with an accurate picture of a student's problems you must keep records of all inappropriate behavior. This documentation will enable you to give a professional, nonjudgmental account of a student's behavior.

Early in the school year, your experience and intuition will guide you in singling out the students who are potential behavior problems. They will let themselves be known by committing minor infractions of the rules. It is vital that you begin documenting their action immediately. Having anecdotal records will be necessary when you seek the support of administrators and parents.

Effective teachers whom we have studied use any of the following methods for documenting student behavior:

- A small notebook with one page per student. (This type of book can be carried to other areas throughout the school.)

- A 3x5 index card, alphabetically arranged in a file, for each student.

- A loose-leaf notebook with one or more pages per student. (This is especially useful for a class with many difficult students.)

An anecdotal record should include the following:

Student's name and class
Date, time and place of incident
Description of rule broken
Disciplinary action taken

Example - Small Notebook

Lois Simon   Grade 4

Date/Time	Place	Rule Broken	Action Taken
9/15 10:45	Classroom	Refused to return to seat	Warning
9/15 1:20	Classroom	Running in class	Lose 10 minutes recess
9/15 1:40	Classroom	Called out without raising hand	Lose 20 minutes recess
9/18 2:00	Hallway	Ran out of line for drink of water	Warning
9/18 2:40	Gym	Continued playing after whistle blew	No gym next week

Example - 3x5 Index Card

Sally Johnson Grade 6 Room 303

10/8   No homework
10/10   Did not hand in spelling test
10/11   No homework
10/12   Did not hand in reading
          assignment
10/13   No Homework

Anecdotal records can also be maintained for poor academic work.

TIP
Keep all student work in a file or in folders. When meeting with parents present the individual file so that parents can see what work their child has or has not completed.

39

Example - Loose-Leaf Notebook

John Doe   Grade 2

10/1, 10:15, John and Alex had a fight. I separated them and John started screaming. I told him to go to his seat and he cussed at me. I sent him to the principal's office.

10/5, 1:45, John punched Jane in the arm. I told him to go to the back of the room to calm down. He started screaming and ran out of the room. I notified the principal and arranged a meeting with the guidance counselor.

10/6, noon, John had a fight in the lunchroom. An aide sent him to an empty bench. He hit the aide. He was removed from the lunchroom and his mother was called immediately.

WORKSHEET - Anecdotal Record

Name _____ Grade _____

Date/Time   Place   Rule Broken   Action Taken

When you have a conference with parents, present the anecdotal records.

- Parents can see the specific behaviors their child engaged in.
- There will be no room to question how you handled the situation.
- There will be no chance for your word to be pitted against a student's.
- You and the parents can address specific problems and devise solutions.

In severe cases, the anecdotal record will show that the student has been given due process and will justify:

- Intervention of principal
- Removal of child from your class into another class
- Referral to counselor or therapist
- Suspension
- Removal to another school

REMEMBER: Having specific records of a student's misdemeanors will enable you to hold a more effective parent-teacher conference. You will feel confident knowing you did everything you could to deal with the problem yourself. You will not be flustered and will not have to rely on your memory.

42

PROCEDURE

V

CONTACT PARENTS AT THE FIRST SIGN OF A PROBLEM

CONTACT PARENTS AT THE FIRST SIGN OF A PROBLEM

The previous four procedures should be incorporated into your daily routine. By following them consistently you will have established positive communication with parents, enabling you to gain their support when you need it.

Procedure 5 presents skills that are designed to be utilized before, during and after you contact parents. On the following pages you will learn:

1. When to Contact Parents
2. How to Contact Parents
3. How to Communicate Assertively
4. How to Improve Verbal Skills
5. How to Maintain Parent Communication Records
6. How to Provide Positive Support For Parents
7. How to Conduct Routine Parent Conferences.

1. When to Contact Parents

IF A PROBLEM ARISES THAT YOU CANNOT HANDLE ON YOUR OWN, CONTACT THE PARENTS AND ASSERT YOURSELF IMMEDIATELY!

Don't wait until routine parent-conference time to discuss major problems with parents. Waiting until this time is ineffective for one of two reasons:

Springing bad news on unsuspecting parents places the teacher as well as the parent in an awkward situation
or
The parents of the most difficult students often don't show up at parent conferences.

Therefore, it is imperative that you exercise your right to parental support the MOMENT A PROBLEM SURFACES that you cannot handle on your own.

REMEMBER: THE FIRST WEEK IS NOT TOO SOON TO CONTACT PARENTS.

Problems Requiring Contact with Parents

Your professional judgment is your best guide in determining when it is necessary to contact parents. A general rule of thumb is that if your typical discipline approach has not brought about any changes for a period of one week, it is time to place a phone call or write a letter to the parents. The exception is if you are using a discipline plan for which a consequence for breaking a rule is a phone call home. In that case you will have to call the parent the moment the rule is broken, not wait a week.

Face-to-face conferences should be reserved for more serious misbehavior. Use the following guidelines for determining the necessity of scheduling a parent-teacher conference:

- Writing to the parent doesn't produce results.

- Phoning the parent doesn't produce results

- There is a severe infraction of the rules (for instance, persistant fighting).

- The student absolutely refuses to conform to classroom procedures.

- The student exhibits bizarre or unusual behavior.

2. How to Contact Parents

When a student has a problem in school, teachers, as was just discussed, typically write a letter or call the parent at home. If the parent cannot be reached, is uncooperative or does not respond to the letter, many teachers simply give up.

CAUTION: DO NOT LET THE ISSUE SLIDE!

The problem is bound to get worse, and you will find yourself losing control and becoming more frustrated in the classroom.

It may be necessary to inconvenience parents in order to impress upon them your need for their help. The two best ways to reach parents who do not return your phone calls or ignore your notes are to:

CALL THE PARENT AT WORK

If you can't reach a parent at home, call him or her at work. Parents do not appreciate being called at work, and will often agree to support you to avoid being called again. Don't hesitate to tell the supervisor that it is extremely important that you speak with the parent. That may be the only way to get the parent to come to the phone.

CALL THE OTHER PARENT

Teachers generally call the mother when there is a problem. But if that doesn't prove successful, call the father. In other words, if one parent isn't cooperative, call the other one. Often one parent in a family is more lenient than the other. It may be necessary to appeal to the "tougher" parent for help. In the case of divorce, it may be necessary to call the parent who lives apart from the child. Divorced parents often feel overwhelmed and uncomfortable about dealing firmly with their children. Others are just too busy to spend time disciplining.

Other Ways to Contact Parents

Send a registered letter or a mailgram. Having a postman deliver a registered letter emphasizes the importance of your message and has an enormous impact. It also prevents a parent from saying he or she never received your communique.

Call the emergency number. Some families may not have a telephone, but the school has on record an emergency number for each child. Usually it is the number of a friend or relative in the same building or down the street. Calling this number is an effective method for reaching the parent. When the neighbor rings the doorbell to say the school is having a problem with their child, the parents will usually respond immediately.

If you are still unsuccessful contacting parents, you should seek administrative support. But before you do, recheck your efforts:

- ☐ Have you phoned parents at home?
- ☐ Have you phoned parents at work?
- ☐ Have you sent a note home requesting a conference?
- ☐ Have you sent a second note home, perhaps with a sibling or neighbor's child?

When you have exhausted all means of reaching the parents, it is time to request intervention from your administrator.

Present details of the problem you are having with the child together with records of your attempts to contact parents. The administrator can then use his or her influence to insist upon a conference.

REMEMBER: To have its greatest effect, an administrator's clout should always be reserved for the most serious issues and only as a last resort.

DO EVERYTHING POSSIBLE TO CONTACT PARENTS WHEN YOU NEED HELP

3. How to Communicate Assertively

Once you do contact the parent, you must communicate in an assertive manner. To do so, assume a take-charge attitude and write or speak in a clear, firm and direct manner.

> **REMEMBER, YOUR UNDERLYING ASSUMPTION FOR ALL COMMUNICATION WITH PARENTS MUST BE: "I HAVE A RIGHT TO PARENTAL SUPPORT. I CANNOT DO MY JOB ALONE."**

The key to your success in gaining parental support over the phone or in person is to BE PREPARED. Think through the way in which you will elicit parental support before you place the call or meet with parents. Having a plan of action will enable you to clearly and firmly communicate to parents what you expect them to do.

Your plan of action should include the following:

Goals for the phone call or conference - Know exactly what you want from parents before you speak to them: "Mrs. Jones, I need your cooperation in regard to your son's fighting in school."

Objectives - Know exactly what you need parents to do to achieve that goal: "Mrs. Jones, I need you to discipline your son whenever I send home a note saying that he's been fighting in school."

Rationale - The following rationale is often used in conversations regarding behavior: "Mrs. Jones, it is in your child's best interest that we work together to eliminate this fighting problem. You and your husband are the most important people in your child's life. You have more influence over him than I ever will. Your influence is vital in helping him. He needs to know we are working together, and that we will do all we can to see that he improves his behavior."

Consequences - State the logical consequences if the problem remains unsolved: "Mrs. Jones, if your son's fighting problem is allowed to continue, I'm afraid he will be suspended from school."

Let's follow the same format to illustrate how you can formulate a plan of action for a phone call to a parent whose child is doing poorly academically.

Goal: Ms. Smith, Gail is having a difficult time learning her multiplication tables. I need you to help her learn them.

Objective: I will send home a pack of cards with different multiplication facts each week. I need you to drill her for 15 minutes each night.

Rationale: We must work together to impress upon her the importance of this skill for her education. She needs to know that you care, as much as I do, that she learn these facts.

Consequence: If she fails to learn the multiplication tables, she will have a great deal of difficulty learning more complicated mathematical skills later on.

> TIP
> Write down the goals, objectives, rationale and consequences for each phone call and conference. Doing so will help you keep the conversation on target if a parent tries to sidetrack you.

54

WORKSHEET - Preparation for Phone Call or Conference

Student's Name _____ Class _____

Reason for Calling Parents

_____

Statement of Goal
I need your help in _____ .

Statement of Objectives

Whenever I _____ , I need you to
_____ .

Rationale
It is in your child's best interest that we work together to _____
_____ .

Consequence

If _____ doesn't _____ ,
I will have no choice but to _____ .

The following guidelines will further enhance your ability to communicate assertively.

Do's:

- Begin with a positive statement about the child.
  > Your son is a leader in the class.
  > Your daughter is an excellent math student.
  > She always looks neat and well-dressed.
  > He's a great basketball player.

- State the problem in specific terms.
  > In the past two weeks, your daughter has been late to school six times.
  > Your son does not do his work. He spends too much time talking to a neighbor.
  > She comes to school unprepared every day - no pencils, paper, books or homework.
  > He had a fight in the cafeteria on Monday and a fight in the yard on Wednesday.

- When appropriate, offer the parent assistance in disciplining his or her child.*
  > I suggest he not be allowed to play with his friends until his work is done.
  > I suggest she be grounded for weekends until her grades improve.
  > I suggest he can't go to the movies if you receive a note from me.
  > I suggest you disconnect her phone until she begins doing her work every night.

- Ask parents how they will reward their child's appropriate behavior. If necessary, make some suggestions.
  > The child can stay up late one night.
  > The child can go to the movies.
  > The parent can take the child for a special lunch.

---

*Refer to Lee Canter's *Assertive Discipline for Parents* for assisting parents in the discipline of their children at home.

Remember, the goal of your call or conference is to solve a problem. Once the issue is resolved, both you and the parent must positively reinforce the child to assure his or her continued success.

- Address the parent by name many times and, if talking in person, look him or her in the eye during a conference.

    By looking into a person's eyes and addressing him or her by name, you are giving assurance that the person has your complete interest and undivided attention. It also shows your sincerity and concern for his or her well-being.

- Summarize the conversation at the end and reiterate what you and the parent agreed to do. If necessary, have the parent repeat the agreement.

    As we agreed, I will send home a note every time your daughter is late for class and you will discipline her at home.

- End the conversation on a positive note.

    I'm sure together we can work this out.
    I feel confident that the problem will be solved.
    I think your daughter will show great improvement with the plan we've agreed upon.

- Follow up on conferences with a note or a phone call.

Dont's:

- Don't apologize for bothering the parent.

  I'm really sorry you had to come to school tonight. (Why should a teacher apologize when feeling concern over an important issue about the child?)

- Don't minimize the problem.

  There's a small problem with Johnny. (In truth, the problem may be very serious, one that is potentially harmful to another child and disruptive to the class.)

- Don't belittle your abilities.

  I'm having such a hard time. I really don't know what to do with him. (Of course you know what is needed. You need the cooperation of the parent in disciplining his or her child. Remember, you can't do it alone.)

- Don't downgrade the consequences of the child's behavior.

  I don't know what will happen to him. (When in reality you do know what will happen. The child may be suspended or fail the subject.)

TIP
Don't hold a conference if you are not prepared for it. If a parent enters the class during the day for an unscheduled visit, greet him or her pleasantly, but suggest another time for a conference. Explain that you want to give him or her your full attention and can only do so when the class is not present.

Assertive Phrases

When speaking with a difficult parent, it is easy to become flustered and lose your train of thought. Use any of these phrases to assert your authority.

I have a right to your help.

It is in your child's best interest that we work together to solve this problem.

I need your support.

I cannot do this job alone.

You are the most important person in your child's life.

I need you to take stronger disciplinary action at home.

If this problem isn't solved, it could lead to greater problems later on.

I will be involved with your child for 10 months of his life. You will be in the picture a lot longer.

I understand, but... .

Your child is your responsibility 24 hours a day.

TIP
When talking to parents:
Stay calm
Speak slowly
Keep it short
Don't become defensive or angry

To further illustrate how to communicate with parents, here is an example of an assertive conference.

Teacher: I'm glad you could come to school today, Ms. Jones. There are some important issues we need to discuss about Andy. By the way, did you notice that wonderful painting of a space station when you walked in? Andy did that. He's an excellent artist, you know. *(Begin with a positive statement.)*

Ms. Jones: He always did like to paint. But he doesn't do much of anything anymore.

Teacher: I've noticed some changes in him, too. That's what we need to discuss. He rarely completes any assignments. When he should be working he sits and talks to his neighbors or plays with small toys he brings from home. *(State the problem in specific terms.)*

Ms. Jones: What can I do about it?

Teacher: A lot. I need your cooperation in working out a solution to Andy's problem. *(State your goal.)* Every day I will send home a note indicating if Andy has or has not completed his work. If he hasn't completed his work I want you to see that he does it at home. *(State your objective.)*

Ms. Jones: But he doesn't listen to me anymore. He does whatever he wants. Nothing I do works!

Teacher: I understand that it isn't easy, Ms. Jones, but you will have to take a firmer stance at home if he refuses to do his work in school. I suggest you not allow him to watch TV until his work is finished. *(Offer the parent assistance in disciplining the child.)*

Ms. Jones: But I'm too tired to argue with him every night.

Teacher: I'm sure you are, but we have to help Andy make some changes. If he continues to neglect his work, he is in jeopardy of failing this year. *(State the consequence.)*

Ms. Jones: Okay.

Teacher: So then, Ms. Jones, do you agree to see that Andy completes his schoolwork at home? *(Summarize the conversation.)*

Ms. Jones: Yes, I agree.

Teacher: Good. Now, Ms. Jones, when Andy does his schoolwork, I suggest you remember to praise him and occasionally provide some special treat. *(Suggest a reward for appropriate behavior.)*

Ms. Jones: Well, that should be easy.

Teacher: (smiling) Ms. Jones, I will explain our plan to Andy and send home the first note tomorrow. I am sure if we work at this, we can help Andy achieve better grades and improve his behavior both at school and at home. Thank you for coming to school today. *(End on positive note.)*

The outcome of this conference is constructive. It will produce results.

The teacher's needs were met: She let the parent know she couldn't do her job alone.

The parent's needs were met: She received suggestions in coping with her son's problem.

The child's needs were met: It was in his best interest that he be more firmly supervised.

The assertive teacher was in full command. She had the attitude, "I have a right to parental support." She was prepared for the meeting, proved her concern for the child and offered concrete solutions to the problem.

CHECKLIST — For Parent-Teacher Conferences

☐ Will there be complete privacy? (Interruptions should be avoided. No children or other adults should be present.)

☐ Is the conference site comfortable? Provide adult-sized chairs. DO NOT SIT AT SMALL DESKS ON SMALL CHAIRS.

☐ Are all records at your fingertips?

   ☐ Anecdotal records

   ☐ Past class records

   ☐ Report cards

   ☐ Health records (if necessary)

   ☐ Other pertinent data

☐ Have you selected samples of the student's work (good as well as unsatisfactory) to show the parents?

☐ Have you written the goals, objectives, rationale and consequences for the conference?

☐ Do you have a copy of the discipline plan letter that was signed by the parent?

62

An Alternative to Phoning or Meeting with Parents.

An alternative to phoning or meeting with parents is to communicate problems to them by writing a letter. This is the least desirable form of contact because it is a one-sided effort - it permits no interaction or give and take. However, if writing a letter is more convenient for you, use the technique with caution and keep in mind the following guidelines:

- A letter about a problem should never be the first piece of mail a parent receives from you. You should already have written at least one positive note home.

- The problem you are writing about should be in the early stages, not something severe.

- In the letter, state the problem in straightforward terms -avoid opinions or judgments.

- Mention a specific way in which the problem can be solved.

- Request that the parent answer your letter.

Example: Letter

Dear Mrs. Richards:

I am writing to inform you about a problem that appears to be developing with Eric in school.

Yesterday he took Julie's book without her permission.

Today he put paint on her paper and she became very upset.

I changed his seat, hoping that would solve the problem.

At this time I think it will be sufficient for you to simply talk to him about it, but if the problem continues, I will call you and we will work out the solution together.

Please let me know the outcome of your discussion with Eric.

Sincerely,
Miss Smith

4. How to Improve Verbal Skills

At certain times you may find you are unsuccessful gaining support of difficult parents when using the aforementioned techniques. For those instances we would like to give you some specific verbal techniques to use during phone conversations or conferences.

Broken Record

The broken-record technique is one of the most important skills you can learn in becoming more assertive with parents. It is so-named because you will sound like a broken record when you use it. It works well with:

- Parents who try to sidetrack the issue
- Parents who try to blame you for their child's problems
- Parents who make excuses for their children

You can counteract their resistance to supporting you by simply repeating a statement of your goal for the conference. Preface the statement with:

I understand, but... .

Teacher:	Mr. Brown, **I need you to see that Allan does his homework every night.** *(Goal)*
Mr. Brown:	Look, this job I'm on now is a killer. By the end of the day I'm really too tired to argue over homework.
Teacher:	I understand, but **I need you to see that he does his homework every night."** *(Broken record)*
Mr. Brown:	But I need some peace and quiet at night. I have this new boss who hounds me all day. All I want to do when I get home is eat some dinner and relax.
Teacher:	I understand, but **I need you to see that he does his homework every night.** *(Broken record)*
Mr. Brown:	You sure are persistant, Okay, I'll see that he does it.

65

In most cases you will only need to repeat yourself three times before the parent knows you mean business. However, if after three times the parent is still unwilling to bend, offer him or her a choice - to cooperate with you or accept the inevitable consequence.

Teacher: Mrs. Evans, **I need your help in disciplining Amy.** *(Goal)*

Mrs. Evans: But I don't like to punish her; she gets so upset.

Teacher: I understand that you don't enjoy punishing her, but **I need your help in disciplining her.** *(Broken record)*

Mrs. Evans: But she starts to cry whenever I scold her.

Teacher: I understand, but **I need your help in disciplining her."** *(Broken record)*

Mrs. Evans: I want my children to love me, not to hate me.

Teacher: I really understand how difficult it is for you, but you have a choice. Either you begin disciplining Amy or the school will be forced to retain her another year. *(Offer a choice.)* Her poor behavior is causing her to fall far behind the rest of the class. If she doesn't show some improvement soon, she will have to repeat third grade.

Mrs. Evans: It's really serious, isn't it? I guess you do need my help. What would you like me to do?

Wrong Person Technique

Some parents will try to shift the responsibility for their child's poor behavior onto your shoulders. They will make it seem as though you, rather than their child, are the one causing the problem. The "wrong person" technique applies in those cases.

Teacher: If Danny chooses to continue to misbehave, I will be forced to keep him after school.

Ms. Miller: Wait just a minute. You can't do that. If you keep him after school, he'll miss the bus. Then I'll have to leave work to pick him up. If I don't work, I don't get paid.

Teacher: Ms. Miller, **you're talking to the wrong person.** If you don't want to miss work, you'll have to talk to Danny about that.

Teacher: Debbie broke a class rule three times today. Therefore she will have to stay 45 minutes after school tomorrow.

Mrs. Shaw: I'm sorry, but you can't have Debbie stay late tomorrow. She has a piano lesson.

Teacher: Mrs. Shaw, **you're talking to the wrong person.** If Debbie does not want to stay after school, she will have to learn to follow the school rules.

Active Receiving and Sending of Messages

Whenever communication takes place there is always the question of whether each party understands what the other is saying. Often a parent may not have heard what you actually said and vice versa. To avoid confusion and assure that the message was properly transmitted, you may need to clarify all statements. You can do this by rephrasing the parent's words and having the parent rephrase yours. We call this active receiving and sending of messages.

Mr. Lawson: I'll go home tonight and come up with some way of disciplining Jack.

Teacher: Let me see if I understand you correctly. At home tonight, you will come up with a specific plan for disciplining your son. *(Active receiving)*

Mr. Lawson: That's right.

Teacher: You'll let me know by Thursday the specific disciplinary action you will take whenever I write a note saying your son misbehaved in class.

Mr. Lawson: Okay.

Teacher: I'd like to make sure we understand each other. What did you hear me saying? *(Active sending)*

Mr. Lawson: By Thursday, you want to know exactly what I intend to do whenever Jack misbehaves in class.

Teacher: Great. I feel confident we can work out this problem.

Yes-or-No Technique

This technique forces a commitment from parents who are reluctant to promise you their support. Such parents respond in vague, non-committal terms to your request for help. ("I'll think about it." "I'll see what I can do." "Maybe. I'll consider it.")

If you do not pursue the issue, you will be left up in the air with no commitment, pro or con, from the parents. Such a response during a phone call or conference would be a waste of time. Therefore you must assert yourself and ask the parent to take a stand: "Yes, I will support you," or, "No, I will not."

Mrs. Johnson: I'm not sure I'll be able to do what you ask. I'll have to see if I have time.

Teacher: I hear you saying that you won't check Bill's homework every night.

Mrs. Johnson: No, I'm just not sure if I'll be able to.

Teacher: Mrs. Johnson, it's in your son's best interest that we both do our part in improving his academic standing. **I need to know - yes or no -** will you help him at home?

Mrs. Johnson: Well, If you insist. Okay, yes, I'll look at his homework every night.

68

> **TIP**
> In cases where parents are reluctant to promise their support, follow up the conversation with a letter to the parent reiterating what was said.

Mrs. Newman: I'm not sure I'll be able to do what you suggest. Jenny makes such a fuss when I ground her after school.

Teacher: I hear you saying that you will not ground Jenny when she misbehaves.

Mrs. Newman: No. I'm just not sure I will be able to follow through with the punishment if she carries on about it.

Teacher: Mrs. Newman, Jenny will continue to misbehave in school as long as she can talk you out of any punishment you try to enforce. It is in your daughter's best interest that you take a firmer stand in disciplining her. **I need to know - yes or no -** will you ground her if I tell you she has misbehaved in class?

Mrs. Newman: I guess you're right; I should be stricter. Okay, yes, I'll ground her.

The following dialogue from a parent-teacher-principal conference illustrates the skills we have just presented. Each communication technique used throughout the conversation is clearly labeled.

Principal: Thank you for coming to school today, Mr. Reynolds. We are encountering some serious problems with Susan and we need your cooperation in dealing with them. *(State your goal.)*

Mr. Reynolds: I'd like to know exactly why I had to come to school today? We could have discussed this on the phone.

Principal: Mrs. Edison, Susan's homeroom teacher has called you a number of times, but it hasn't helped.

69

Teacher: Mr. Reynolds, I called you on October 23rd and October 30th. *(Refer to parent communication records.)* But Susan is still cutting class. *(State the problem.)*

Mr. Reynolds: That's impossible. I spoke with her about that and she promised to stop.

Teacher: Well she hasn't. She cut Math class on Tuesday and English on Friday. *(Show documentation.)* As a result, her grades are dropping.

Mr. Reynolds *(reading documentation):*
I really thought she was doing better.

Principal: That is why we asked you to come to school. Mr. Reynolds, we need you to take stronger action whenever Susan cuts class.

Mr. Reynolds: Look, I really can't handle her any more. Ever since her mother and I were divorced, Susan just can't be controlled.

Principal: I understand. It's not easy. But we need you to take stronger action when she cuts class. *(Broken record)*

Mr. Reynolds: Can't the school do anything about her?

Principal: We would be happy to work with you in solving the problem. But it is in Susan's best interest that you exert more authority with her. *(State the rationale.)*

Teacher: If Susan doesn't straighten out quickly, I'm afraid the problem will become even greater. She may have to repeat 8th grade. *(State the consequence.)*

Mr. Reynolds: It's really serious, isn't it? What can I do?

Teacher: Well to begin with, she needs to be given some meaningful disciplinary consequences for cutting class. Are there any privileges that she especially likes?

Mr. Reynolds: She loves being with her friends and going to parties. I guess I could ground her and not let her go out on the weekend. But I don't know, that's awfully strict.

Principal: Mr. Reynolds, I'm not sure if I understand you correctly. Are you going to take away her weekend privileges? Yes or no. *(Yes-no technique)*

Mr. Reynolds: Okay, yes. I'll ground her. But just for the weekend.

Teacher: Mr. Reynolds, we need you to agree to cooperate with us anytime she cuts class. It's for her own good. Whenever I contact you regarding her misbehavior, I need you to promise to discipline her. *(State the objective.)*

Mr. Reynolds: Okay, I'll do that. I guess maybe I've been too lenient with her all along.

Principal: Susan will be much better off if you provide stronger consequences for her poor behavior. We will keep you informed of her progress. One last point. When Susan starts to show improvement, how do you intend to let her know how pleased you are? *(Suggest a reward for appropriate behavior.)*

Mr. Reynolds: Hmm, let's see. She's been asking for a larger allowance. I could increase it.

Principal: Great idea. And be sure to let Susan know your plan. Thank you for this productive meeting, Mr. Reynolds. I feel confident that things will improve.

Within one month Susan showed marked improvement in her behavior. Her classwork was more acceptable too. The teacher made a point to call Mr. Reynolds to positively reinforce his efforts. The following conversation ensued:

Teacher: Hello, Mr. Reynolds. This is Susan's homeroom teacher. I'm calling to thank you for your cooperation in dealing with Susan's problems. She hasn't missed one class this week and her other teachers report a change in her attitude toward school.

Mr. Reynolds: Well, it wasn't easy. She put up a tough fight - tears, yelling, lots of arguments. But I held firm.

Teacher: It seems to have been well worth the effort.

Mr. Reynolds: I must admit, things are a lot better at home. Susan is more cooperative around the house. She comes home on time and does all her chores. I truly appreciate your guidance and help.

71

REMEMBER: Follow up on all phone calls and conferences.

If the child shows improvement, let the parent know how pleased you are.

If the child is still a problem, don't avoid the issue. Call the parent, arrange a meeting, or come up with another plan.

5. How to Maintain Parent Communication Records

Keep written records of all communication with parents. If a parent **does not** support you as he or she agreed to, you will have specific documentation of notes sent home, conversations that took place and actions agreed upon. Such records will be important to you when confronting an uncooperative parent or appealing for administrative support. You will be able to discuss the matter in a calm and confident manner, referring to your notes to back up your words.

In the office of successful businessmen and women, you will find volumes of records of every phone call and meeting they've had. Most business deals are built on the input of many people, and a human being cannot possibly store all that information in his or her head. Likewise, in education you are in contact with dozens of people each day - students, administrators, colleagues, and parents. It's an impossible task to remember the details of a note sent home, a call you placed or a meeting you had without keeping accurate records.

It really doesn't take much time. Simply jot down one sentence or a short phrase on an index card or in a notebook.

Parent records should include the following:

- Student's name, class
- Parents' names
- Home, work and emergency phone numbers
- Dates of notes sent home regarding poor behavior and poor work habits
- Dates of phone conversations with parents, what the teacher said, what the parent agreed to do
- Dates of notes sent home asking parents to come to school for a conference, parent's response
- All notes received from parents

Example: Parent Records

Carol Simon   Period 3

10/12   Carol cut math class.
        Phoned Mr. S. He will
        not let her go out with
        friends if it happens
        again.

10/20   Carol cut class. Sent note
        to Mr. S.

10/24   Carol cut class. Sent note
        to Mr. S. to come to school
        for conference. No response.

10/26   Phoned mother. Not home —
        did not return call.

10/30   Sent another note. No response.

11/2   Principal sent note to Mr.
        S. Conference scheduled
        11/10.

WORKSHEET - Parent Record Form

Student's name _____ Class _____

Parents' names _____

Home phone# _____ Work phone# _____

Emergency# _____

Discipline plan letter sent (date) _____

Positive notes sent _____ , _____ , _____

Phoned parent _____

    Objective _____

    Parent agreed to _____

Conference date _____

    Objective _____

    Parent agreed to _____

Principal notified (date) _____

Counselor notified (date) _____

> **TIP**
> Keep copies of notes you sent home and notes you received from parents in the student's folder.

> **TIP**
> Send home a written account of your discussion with parents. Certain parents may forget the discipline action they've agreed to take. Seeing it in writing serves as an excellent reminder.

WRITE EVERYTHING DOWN

DO NOT LEAVE ANYTHING TO YOUR MEMORY. CONFIDENCE COMES WITH KNOWING YOU'VE DONE EVERYTHING POSSIBLE AND HAVING RECORDS TO PROVE IT!

6. How to Provide Positive Support For Parents

Remember, just like students, parents need positive reinforcement, too.

Therefore, when a parent **does** what he or she agreed to do, and the child shows improvement, again, it is important to show your pleasure.

Most parents never receive positive feedback from teachers. They are accustomed to hearing from the school only when there is a problem. They are rarely notified when their disciplinary efforts at home are successful.

You can further create a positive atmosphere in your classroom by sending home a note or making a quick phone call to thank a parent for his or her efforts. You will have a much easier time approaching that parent if a problem arises again.

Examples of Positive Notes

Dear Mr. Jackson:
Your son has had perfect attendance all month. Thank you for cooperating with the school and for supervising him more closely. I know he will have an excellent year.
Sincerely,
Ms. Meyer

Dear Ms. Frank,
I want to thank you for all the effort you have taken to discipline Lynn. Her behavior has improved 100%.
Sincerely,
M. Conway

Positive Phone Call Example

Teacher:	Hello, Mrs. Stone. This is Ellen's teacher. I'm calling to tell you that since we spoke two weeks ago, Ellen has handed in a homework assignment every day.
Mrs. Stone:	Well I took your suggestions. She may not go out to play with her friends until her assignments are complete. It's amazing how quickly she does her work now.
Teacher:	I'm so glad. Her work has improved greatly, and I have you to thank. I really appreciate how cooperative you've been.
Mrs. Stone:	You're welcome. But I should be thanking you for taking the time to help me straighten her out. Let me know if you have any other problems with her.

7. How to Conduct Routine Parent Conferences

If you've followed the preceding steps, routine parent conferences will be just that - routine. The meetings will be easy and pleasant for both you and the parent.

REMEMBER: PARENTS SHOULD NOT RECEIVE ANY NEGATIVE SURPRISES DURING PARENT CONFERENCE TIME OR ON REPORT CARDS. MAJOR BEHAVIORAL AND ACADEMIC PROBLEMS SHOULD HAVE BEEN BROUGHT TO THEIR ATTENTION THE MOMENT THEY OCCURRED.

Routine Parent-Conference Time Should Be Used to:

- Update parents on their child's progress in school.

- Discuss the child's strengths.

- Discuss minor behavioral problems.

- Offer parents specific suggestions to improve weak academic areas.

- Explain your grading procedure.

- Explain ambiguous categories on report cards such as, "Work Habits," "Social Skills," "Initiates Projects."

- Allow parents to air any concerns or problems they have regarding their child.

- Inform parents of any upcoming projects or new curriculm you are planning to introduce.

Do's for Routine Parent Conferences

- Arrive at the conference site before the parent.
- Greet the parent warmly.
- Usher the parent to the seat you've selected.
- Look the parent in the eyes when speaking.
- Address the parent often by name.
- Mention some commendable trait about the child early in the conference.
- Hand the parent the child's work to look over. Refer to points which should be noted.
- End the conference on time, and schedule another one if needed.
- Make detailed notes of what was discussed.

Dont's for Routine Parent Conferences

- Don't surprise parents with new problems. Parents should be notified the moment a problem arises.
- Don't make small talk. Use every moment of the parent's time to discuss the student's progress.
- Don't do all the talking. You do want to maintain control of the conference, but you should allow the parent to discuss his or her concerns and ideas. You may learn an important piece of information that can be useful in helping the child.

PROCEDURE VI

WHEN ALL ELSE FAILS

WHEN ALL ELSE FAILS

In the preceding chapters were suggestions that will work with 98% of the parents you encounter. The remaining 2% are the toughest to handle, and you may need to employ additional techniques with these parents to ensure their cooperation. These parents can be classified into two categories:

- Parents who absolutely refuse to share the responsibility for their children from 9:00 to 3:00

- Parents who are outwardly hostile to educators and to the school system in general

Experience demonstrates that the best way to deal with difficult parents is to provide consequences for the child that will make it as "inconvenient" for the parents as possible. These consequences should always be offered to the parents as a choice. For example: "Mrs. Williams, you have a choice. Either you discipline your daughter when she misbehaves in school, or I will be forced to call you at work every single time she breaks a rule." The important thing to remember is you must be willing to follow through with the consequence and use it consistently until the parent agrees to support you.

What follows are methods that can be used with severely disruptive students and difficult parents.

ONE KEY QUALIFIER: DO NOT HANDLE THESE PARENTS ALONE. THESE TECHNIQUES SHOULD ALWAYS BE USED WITH ADMINISTRATIVE SUPPORT.

Method 1 - Call the Parent at Work

As we mentioned earlier, calling the parent at work is an effective way to gain parental support. With uncooperative parents you may need to call **three, four,** or **five** times until the parent is inconvenienced enough to be willing to support the school's efforts.

If you have difficulty getting through to the parent, say to the supervisor:
> "This is Mrs. Mason's son's teacher. There is a serious situation concerning her son and I must speak with her immediately."

Or be more specific:
> "Mr. Carson's daughter was involved in a serious fight at school and I must speak to him at once."

If you call every time the student misbehaves, the supervisor is bound to become annoyed and may place pressure on the parent to take action to stop the phone calls.

Method 2 - Take the Child Home or to the Parent's Place of Work.

If calling the parent doesn't produce results, try doing what the principal did in the following situation.

George Remsen was the classic 5th-grade troublemaker. He had been a problem since the beginning of school. His father refused to cooperate when contacted by George's teacher.

One day George threw a chair across the room and missed hitting the head of a fellow student by three inches. The principal, Ms. Burns, was notified. George was removed from class and suspension proceedings began. The principal phoned Mr. Remsen at work.

She spoke first to the supervisor who said Mr. Remsen couldn't come to the phone. Ms. Burns would not be put off. She told the supervisor that there was an emergency at his son's school, Mr. Remsen came to the phone within two minutes.

Principal: This is Ms. Burns, the principal at George's school. Your son was involved in a serious incident today. We need you to come to school immediately and help us work out this problem.

Mr. Remsen: Hey, why are you calling me at work for something like that? I can't come to school now. I've got five more hours on this shift.

Principal: When your son causes problems during our working day, you will have to leave your job and help us solve the problem.

Mr. Remsen: I can't do that. If I leave the factory now, they'll dock my pay.

Principal: Mr. Remsen, you're talking to the wrong person. Every time George chooses to disrupt his class, I'll have to call you and ask you to take him home. If you don't want to be called, I suggest you talk to him about following the rules. He's becoming a serious problem and the school can no longer be responsible for him.

Mr. Remsen: Wait a minute. That kid is your problem from 9:00 till 3:00.

Principal: No, Mr. Remsen. George is your responsibility 24 hours a day. You have a choice. Either you come to school now, or I'll be forced to bring George to you.

Mr. Remsen: Very funny. I'm not leaving work, and I don't want you to call me here ever again.

Principal: You leave me no choice. Goodbye, Mr. Remsen.

With that, the principal took care of some last minute details, ushered George to her car and drove to the father's place of employment. It was a long drive, about 10 miles away, but Ms. Burns was determined to solve the problem of George's behavior once and for all.

87

Ms. Burns marched George into the supervisor's office, told him the situation, and Mr. Remsen was summoned. Seeing his son and Ms. Burns standing next to his angry supervisor was very upsetting to Mr. Remsen. He had no choice. He took his son home and lost a day's pay.

The father in this situation was so greatly inconvenienced that he finally agreed to work with the school to change his son's behavior. At a meeting with the parent, teacher and principal, a contract was formulated to improve George's behavior. Mr. Remsen agreed to provide discipline whenever he received notice that his son was disruptive in school. Rewards for good reports were also agreed upon. The principal, teacher, parent and student all signed the contract. In addition, the school arranged for regular meetings between George and the guidance counselor. Within three weeks the problem was solved.

> **TIP**
> Whenever you need to take severe measures to insure parental support, have the guidance counselor follow up on the home situation. There is always the possibility that the child may be physically abused. Report any suspicion of child abuse to the proper authorities.

Method 3 - Monitoring Student Behavior

Some parents do not believe their child is a serious problem at school. Others absolutely refuse to do anything about it. In these cases, offer parents a choice - either they come to school and monitor their child, or the school will have to suspend the child. If the

88

parent agrees, have him or her sit in on every class with the child, including cafeteria and gym.

To have it's greatest effect, the parent must continue coming to school until the student shows improvement or the parent agrees to help.

This method is sucessful because:

- The parent sees for him or herself exactly how the child behaves in school.
- The parent is usually inconvenienced and eventually agrees to help.
- The student feels pressure from peers about having his or her parent at school and begins to behave.

Method 4 - Detain Students after School

A frequently-used consequence for students who severely mis-behave is to detain them after school. This is particularly effective when students are bussed. A parent who has to leave work to pick up his or her child may be inconvenienced enough to work with the school to improve the child's behavior. Always give parents twenty-four hours notice before using this method.

Method 5 - Truant Students

If a student is continually truant and the parents have not cooperated in solving the problem, offer the parents a choice. They must drive the child to school each morning and escort the child into the building, or the child will be suspended.

REMEMBER: When explaining to parents the methods just mentioned:

- Offer the consequence as a choice.

- Use the "broken record" and other verbal skills to avoid being sidetracked.

- Back up your words with action.

Suggestions for Dealing with Hostile Parents

At some time in your teaching career you may encounter a parent who becomes verbally or physically hostile toward you. Such instances occur when you least expect them. For example, an irate parent may appear at your classroom door after receiving unpleasant news from the school about his or her child. These rare cases should always be handled as an emergency and you must get immediate help!

At a staff meeting, decide the most efficient way of signaling for help when a hostile parent enters a classroom. One suggestion is for teachers to carry a specially designed emergency card (e.g., bright red) with them at all times. This card, when sent to the office, signifies an emergency situation requiring immediate help. Another method is to send a quick note to the principal with the words, "Emergency -Room 211."

Your principal has experience in dealing with these delicate situations. He or she will usher the parent to the office so that you can continue teaching. Once the parent is calm, the principal will be able to address the parent's concerns and suggest a satisfactory solution.

TIP:
Check to see if there are any laws in your state that protect teachers from abuse. In some states it is illegal for parents to threaten a teacher.

TIP:
If you suspect that a certain parent may become hostile during a conference, ask a counselor, another teacher or the principal to be present.

SUMMARY

We have presented you with the guidelines for establishing a total plan for parent communication. Ideally, you should begin this program the first day of school and continue it throughout the year. However, if you are in the middle of the school year and would like to improve your communication with parents now, it can be done. Simply begin by redefining your classroom standards and make known your expectations to your class, your administrator and the parents. Once that is done, start communicating positively with both students and parents. Then the very moment there is a problem, don't wait. Call the parent and in a straightforward, nonjudgmental, assertive manner explain the problem the child is having and what the parents must do to support you.

If you are unsuccessful in gaining their support at first, don't give up. Utilize the skills we present in Procedure V to assert yourself, remembering that you have a right to parental support. It may take some time until you are comfortable with this approach, but once it becomes part of your style you will find that contact with parents is easier than ever before.

A FINAL WORD

Teaching is one of the most gratifying professions a person can choose. You have within your power the ability to inspire and enlighten the young people of our country. In order to do your job and do it well, you need help from parents. Working together as a team, you and the parents can have a positive, long-lasting effect on the child.

In order to gain parental support, you need to develop a good relationship with parents and stay in continual communication with them - not only when their children are doing poorly in school, but when they are doing well.

Remember, your communication with parents should not be limited to routine parent conferences. Whenever you need help, ask for it, and just keep in mind these important points:

> *You have a right to support from parents*
> *and*
> *Be prepared before you meet with parents*

It may take a little extra time and energy, but in the long run your extra effort will be greatly rewarded.

Materials Available From Canter And Associates, Inc.

Product #	Item Description	Unit Price
1009	Assertive Discipline for Parents	$ 7.95
1010	Parent Resource Guide	7.95
1016	Assertive Discipline Text	6.95
1019	Resource Materials Workbook—Secondary	6.95
1024	Resource Materials Workbook—Elementary	6.95
1033	Desktop Motivators—Monthly Positive Activities (gr.1-4)	4.95
1034	Awards for Reinforcing Positive Behavior—Primary	4.95
1035	Awards for Reinforcing Positive Behavior—Intermediate	4.95
1040	Assertive Discipline Teacher Kit—Elementary	49.95
1041	Assertive Discipline Teacher Kit—Secondary	49.95
1042	Bulletin Boards for Reinforcing Positive Behavior—Primary	7.95
1043	Bulletin Boards for Reinforcing Positive Behavior—Intermediate	7.95
1048	Positive Reinforcement Activities—Elementary	5.95
1049	Parent Conference Book	6.95
1052	Positive Reinforcement Activities—Secondary	5.95
1053	Schoolwide Positive Activities	7.95
1063	Teacher Plan Book Plus #2	4.95
1064	Teacher Plan Book Plus	4.95
1071	Wanted for Good Behavior Poster	3.50
1072	Star Tracks Positive Reinforcement Poster	3.50
1073	Classroom Rules Poster—Primary	2.25
1074	Classroom Rules Poster—Intermediate	2.25
1076	Marbles-in-a-Jar Reward Poster (includes 150 marble stickers)	4.95
1083	"I'm an Assertive Teacher" Tote Bag	7.95
1085	"I'm an Assertive Teacher" Mug	4.95

Order from your local school supply dealer.

For information about the materials listed above, or to receive a complete catalogue, write to:
Canter & Associates, Inc.
P.O. Box 2113, Dept. B7
Santa Monica, CA 90406

Sticking sharp metal stars on wood play ground equipment
Talked about problem of kids getting hurt and
he has given me several more.
Concern for Curtis due to his lack of concern or lack of
insight.

We have an obligation to—
  1. Help with parenting
  2. "   develop skills for parenting
        problems at home
            1. be the boss
            2 have rules
            3. Back up words with actions
            4. Be positive

Contacts with Parents

1) must have to attitude that you must have their support
2) Every interaction must convey your concern for their child
3. Must demonstrate professionalism & confidence

Reasons for Homework.
Reinforcement, review, application, enrichment, & home enrollment. limited
, teaching the skill of being accountable

I will check home work.
How home work influences grades.
All in on time completed & ledgeable
Should be students own work.
Approximately how much time?

Establishing Positive Communications with Parents
Document all problems also positive happenings
Contact parents at the first sign of trouble
   a. Don't introduce new problems at conference time

Initial Phone Call — Plan in writing — Do not send double message.
                                           " " " positive message.
   a. Describe behavior
   b. What you have done
   c. What like parents to do
   d. confidence statement
   e. follow up.

After the phone call
   Improved - Thank you

Problem Continued
   Describe behavior
   what you have done
   ask parent to come in
   state concern
   confidence

Face to Face Conference
   Describe Behavior
   what you have done
   state concern
   parental input
   Determine what you will do
                  parent will do

How to Disarm Criticism
   justified - accept it

Unjustified Criticism — focus upon the child
 Listen
 Ask for more information
 If possible, find a point to agree upon
 * Refocus
 (Emphasize

 ↓ I understand + that's not the point

Face to Face

 — Emphasize that you have an answer
 — state what you will do
 — "   "   child needs parent to do
 — Emphasize you are most important person
 — State consequences for child if parent's non-cooperative
 — Use Broken Record to keep focus